Antarctic Journal

Antarctic Journal

Four Months at the Bottom of the World

Jennifer Owings Dewey

SCHOLASTIC INC.

New York Toronto London Auckland Sydney
Mexico City New Delhi Hong Kong Buenos Aires

Photo credits: Pages 8, 13, 16, 28, 29, 47, and 60 © Jennifer Owings Dewey; page 44 © Dr. Robert Greenler; pages 12, 15, 19, 30, 35, 36, 38, 41, 49, and 59 courtesy of the National Science Foundation

ISBN 0-439-38487-7

12 11 10 9 8 7 6 5 4 3   7/0

Printed in the U.S.A.   23

First Scholastic printing, January 2002

Designed by Barbara Balch

To my friend and fellow explorer, C. B.
—J.O.D

November 12th

Depart from home in the early morning, to be gone four months to Antarctica, a part of the planet as remote as the moon in its own way.

The woman sitting next to me on the shuttle is headed for San Antonio, Texas. She has more luggage than I do.

For millions of years Antarctica, the fifth largest continent, has been in the grip of an ice age. It is the windiest, coldest, most forbidding region on earth, and I am heading straight for it.

"Good-bye, America," I whisper as the airplane heaves off the ground with a shuddering roar. "See you later."

November 17th

our ship

We flew from Miami to Santiago, Chile. Early the next morning we boarded a plane bound for Punta Arenas, a town at the southern tip of Chile.

We landed and were driven to a hangarlike building, where we received our Antarctic clothing issue, on loan for the length of our stay, to be returned when we head back.

Our next stop was the pier where the *Polar Duke*, our ship, was tied up.

I was shown to my cabin—a space so tiny, I wished I were an elf. A desk and chair are bolted to the floor. The bedding is a well-padded sleeping bag.

We're off this morning. Clear skies, cool breeze, and no chop. The ship heaves and rolls like the smallish, sturdy seaworthy vessel it is.

wandering albatross

I make a nest
in one of the boats
tied on deck, a cozy
spot to spend hours
drawing or just looking. I resist
going below to sleep or eat. There is
too much to take in—rolling seas, salt
spray, broad-winged seabirds soaring inches
above the wave tops.

sooty albatross

Polar Gear

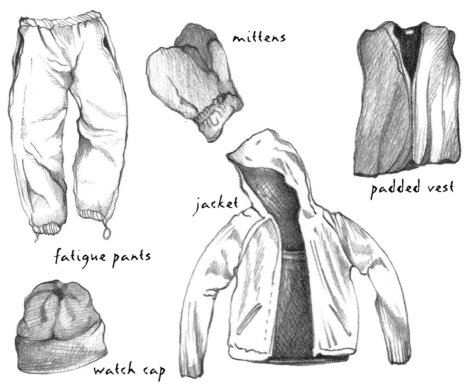

mittens

padded vest

fatigue pants

jacket

watch cap

sea spider

The sun never sets. It
lowers and rolls lazily along the
northern horizon before rising
again. I shiver with anticipation
when we leave the calm waters of the
Beagle Channel and enter Drake Passage.

Two days pass and we cross the Antarctic
Convergence. Along this invisible line warm northern
water meets cold southern water. The layering of warm
and cold, and the upwelling that
results, creates ideal conditions for
an abundance of life in the seas.

From the convergence on, we are
in Antarctica.

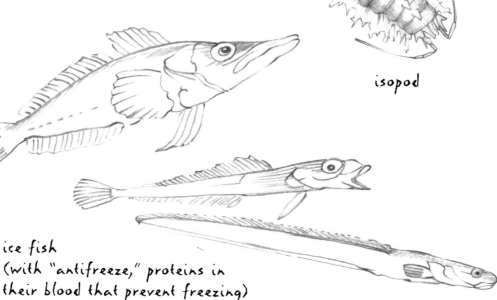

isopod

ice fish
(with "antifreeze," proteins in
their blood that prevent freezing)

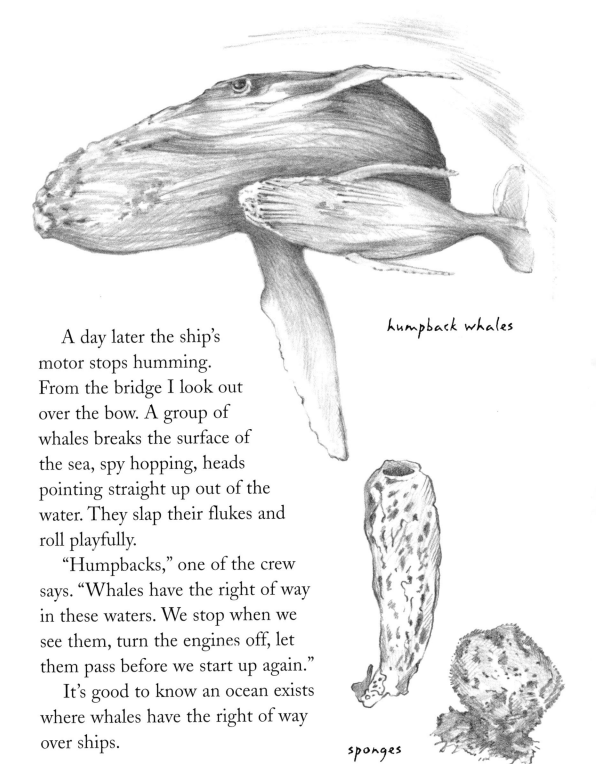

humpback whales

A day later the ship's motor stops humming. From the bridge I look out over the bow. A group of whales breaks the surface of the sea, spy hopping, heads pointing straight up out of the water. They slap their flukes and roll playfully.

"Humpbacks," one of the crew says. "Whales have the right of way in these waters. We stop when we see them, turn the engines off, let them pass before we start up again."

It's good to know an ocean exists where whales have the right of way over ships.

sponges

November 18th
Palmer Station

Dear T.,

Palmer Station is a group of insulated metal buildings, housing fifty people comfortably. The station was built on Anvers Island. You don't know you're on an island because permanent ice fills the gap between Anvers and the mainland.

Palmer Station

my first glimpse of Adélie penguins
on shore in front of Palmer

The science labs are on the first level, with a "mud room" for shedding parkas and wet boots. The dormitories are on the third level, with the kitchen and dining room on the second. Off the dining area is an alcove by a big bay window, a corner set up with stuffed chairs, a sofa, books, and board games like Clue and Monopoly.

View looking away from Palmer

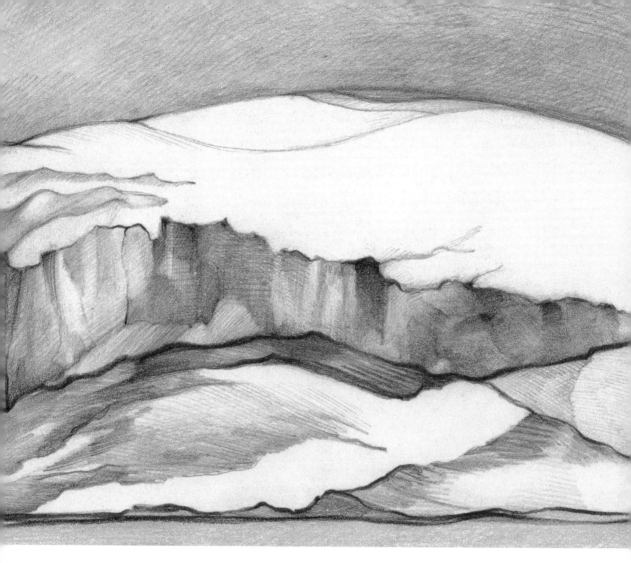

the glacier behind Palmer

My roommate is Polish. She speaks little English. I don't know
Polish, so we use hand signals.

There are upper and lower bunks (I get the upper), a closet, a
sink, and one window. The washroom is down the hall.

We learn the rules the first night: no travel alone, except to
climb the glacier behind Palmer, flagged with poles to show the

safest way up. We sign out when leaving, giving a departure hour and an estimated time of return. We are given walkie-talkies and check with "base" every hour. If we're half an hour off

Typical room, not mine!

schedule, someone comes looking, unless a storm blows in. If it's too dangerous for anyone to come after us, we are expected to wait out the bad weather.

The sunscreen they pass out is "the only kind strong enough." We are ordered never to forget to use it.

Tomorrow we learn about the zodiacs, small rubber boats with outboard motors. I'm excited about what comes next, and sleepy.

Much love,

Antarctic landscape

November 24th
Palmer Station

Adélie penguin

Antarctica

- is five and a quarter million square miles; it's larger than Europe.

- has no native human population.

- contains two thirds of the planet's fresh water in the form of glaciers.

- receives less than two inches of snow or rain in a year (precipitation at the South Pole is barely measurable).

scientists at work

- has no land-based predators (other than humans).

- has one hundred million penguins in residence.

- is a world park, a continent devoted to science, a vast outdoor laboratory.

- has freezing temperatures that keep anything from rotting, even old shacks built by early explorers.

- has ice up to three miles thick, covering ninety-eight percent of the land; in winter the volume of ice doubles along the edge of the continent.

- has bedrock that is depressed two to three thousand feet by the weight of the ice.

- has only one mammal, the Weddell seal (named for an early explorer), that lives there all year long.

- has only two flowering plants: Antarctic hair grass (*Deschampsia antarctica*) and Antarctic pearlwort (*Colobenthos subulatus*).

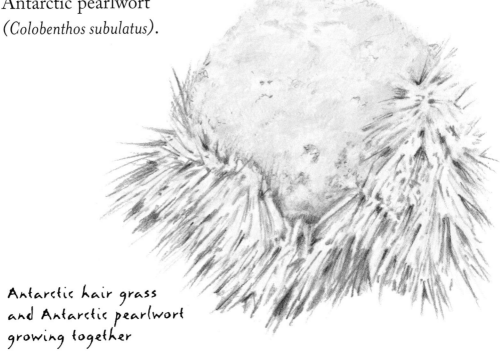

Antarctic hair grass
and Antarctic pearlwort
growing together

November 27th
Litchfield Island

gray gull chick

In fair weather I go to Litchfield Island and spend the day, sometimes the night. Litchfield is three miles from Palmer by zodiac, a protected island visited by two or three people a year. Before going to Litchfield, I'm shown how to walk on open ground in Antarctica. An inch of moss takes one hundred years to grow. The careless scuff of a boot heel could rip out two hundred years of growth in seconds.

OLD PALMER

Litchfield ISLAND →

GLACIER

• PALMER STATION

I pack my food and extra clothes in a waterproof sea bag. A day pack holds pencils, pens, and paper for drawing and writing. There is no fresh water on the island. I carry two one-gallon canteens.

Adélie penguin

Each island has an emergency cache of food and supplies, marked with a flag, available if a person gets stranded during a storm.

Alone after being dropped on the island, I hear birds call, the whine of the wind, the waves pounding gravel shores, and no human sounds except my breathing.

dressed for fieldwork

Twilight falls and I crawl into my tent, alert and unable to sleep for a long time, listening to the sounds of the Antarctic night.

The emergency cache on Litchfield contained a tarp, blankets, rope, candles, matches, anchovy paste, crackers, and chocolate.

December 3rd
Litchfield Island

One of the larger islands offshore, Litchfield has a penguin rookery, or nesting area, on the gently sloping western edge. The ground is rocky but flat enough for penguins to build nests, with a beach close by for gathering small gray nest stones.

The rookery is occupied by two or three hundred penguins. It's small by penguin standards. The penguins are nearly all Adélies, named in 1838 by Dumont d'Urville after his wife. I wonder, did they look like her, act like her, or was he just missing her?

Pairs greet each other at the nest with calls like braying donkeys. They rub breasts and bellies, flap wings, stretch necks, and reach for the sky with their bills—behavior called "ecstatic display."

Adélie penguins greeting each other with the ecstatic display

I find a sheltered perch by the rookery and put my six-pound metal typewriter on a flat rock. The penguins begin to wander over.

They huddle close, smelling of guano and salt water, gently tugging at my clothing with their bills. One bold bird takes my hat and goes off with it.

chinstrap penguin and chicks

They are curious about the tap-tap-tapping noise of the typewriter. They walk up and across it, tugging at the paper tucked into the roller. I let them have their way. Human visitors may not touch penguins, or any wildlife, but the penguins can take their time checking us out.

I follow penguins stone collecting, real work for an Adélie. They carry one stone at a time in their bills. It requires hundreds of trips to complete a nest.

penguins everywhere

Placing a stone takes time. With the stone in its bill, the penguin circles the nest, bowing like a butler. Finally deciding where the stone is needed most, the bird drops it and shuffles away to the beach for another. If one penguin steals a stone from another, a noisy argument erupts. Frustrated birds shriek like squabbling children, but they never come to blows.

Adélie parent and newly hatched chick

Nests sheltering eggs are not left alone. Both parents guard eggs and chicks against foul weather and fierce, predatory skuas.

With eggs in the nest, one partner feeds at sea while the other stays home, keeping the eggs warm under a brood pouch at the base of its belly, a featherless patch of skin with an extra supply of blood vessels.

skua taking a gentoo chick

When hatching begins, the muffled noises of chicks pecking the inner walls of shells join with other sounds. Fluffy chicks appear, round puffballs of gray down.

feeding time

The feeding parent returns from the sea, and after several minutes of ecstatic display, he or she (impossible for me to tell which) steps into the ring of stones and settles on the nest. The bedraggled, guano-stained, empty-bellied partner races for the sea.

Like babies everywhere, penguin chicks gape, mew, squeak, and cry to let the parent in charge know they are hungry. The parent opens its bill, and the chick sticks its head halfway down the gullet. A stream of pink soup spills out. Most of it ends up in the baby's throat; the rest streaks the chick's downy breast. By mid season open ground in the rookery is sloppy with this partly digested krill.

Half the chicks will survive their first winter. The rest will become food for skuas, orcas, and leopard seals.

skua gull stealing a penguin egg

December 6th
Palmer Station

200 million years ago

A little (astonishing) history: Two hundred million years ago, Antarctica had a temperate climate and was part of a supercontinent called Gondwanaland. This vast land mass covered most of the southern hemisphere.

One hundred and seventy million years ago, Antarctica split off from the rest of Gondwanaland. At the same time, mammals began to evolve on Antarctica. The continent drifted over the South Pole, receiving little direct sunlight.

Antarctica grew colder. The strait called Drake Passage opened, allowing circumpolar winds to howl in a twenty-four-thousand-mile circuit around the bottom of the globe. Now winds average forty miles an hour and create waves thirty feet tall.

Today Antarctica is cold, dry, and windy, circled by the earth's stormiest ocean.

170 million years ago

Today

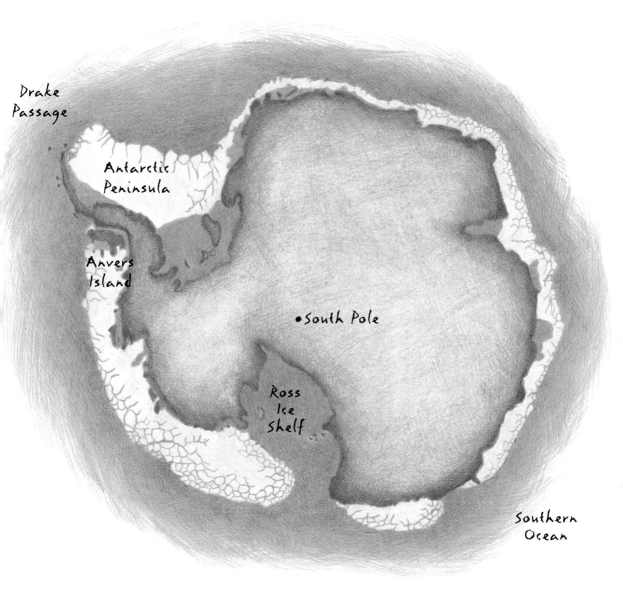

Drake Passage

Antarctic Peninsula

Anvers Island

•South Pole

Ross Ice Shelf

Southern Ocean

Winter temperatures drop to ninety degrees below zero. The Peninsula coastal area is nicknamed the banana belt, because its average temperatures are warmer than inland temperatures.

Antarctica has only one year-round land resident, a mite the size of a pinhead.

December 15th
Visiting Old Palmer

traveling by zodiac

Dear B.,

I am in a tiny office behind the kitchen. Supper is over. I came to find quiet time and write you. It's strange to write at night by the light of the sun.

Today I went with a penguin scientist to Old Palmer, twenty minutes by zodiac from New Palmer. Not used for years, the base is empty of life except for a small colony of gentoo penguins. A few of the birds have built stone nests on top of abandoned oil drums and other debris

gentoo parent
feeding chicks

left behind. The chicks have orange spots on their bills and are identical to the parents, only smaller. They sit half squashed under a parent's white belly, black-billed faces poking out, eyes blinking.

A sunny day, thirty-two degrees, dangerously hot for the chicks. I've seen some keel over dead on days like this, their blubber-rich bodies unable to tolerate temperatures above freezing. A parent penguin suffering heat stroke will not abandon a nest. It will fall dead in a heap first.

gentoos on nests

orca

We had a scary encounter on the way back from Old Palmer. A
pair of orcas were in Arthur Harbor. They swam near the surface,
sleek backs glistening.

These enormous predators sometimes take bites out of boats,
mistaking a zodiac for a seal or a penguin. We slowed the engine
and held back.

A small group of Adélies was porpoising in the water. In a quick stroke one orca grabbed a penguin in its huge mouth and whirled the helpless bird in the air. Teeth gripped penguin flesh, penguin wings flailed. The skin of the penguin flew away and landed with a plop on the sea. The bird was stripped of its hide as easily as we remove a sweater.

young
Adélie

The second orca took a penguin before the pair surged out of the harbor, leaving a swirling wake behind.

We sped back to Palmer, aware that what we'd seen was a reminder that we are in a wilderness where a delicate balance exists between predator and prey.

I'm tired, although I have the BIG EYE. This is when we can't sleep because it's never dark. We get silly and wide-eyed, peculiar in our behavior, until a friend says, "Time for bed," and sees that we get there.

Love and hugs,

J.

orca

December 20th
Palmer Station

blue whales

I have learned that the largest animal on earth, the hundred-ton blue whale, eats only one of the smallest animals on earth: krill (*Euphausia supurba*). There are more krill in the seas than there are stars in the visible universe.

Krill is one link in a simple food chain. Penguins, seals, and whales eat krill. In turn the tiny shrimplike krill eat phytoplankton, one-celled plants that bloom in the sea in spring and summer.

My new friend, Carl, an oceanographer, said we ought to try eating krill since so many animals thrive on it.

In the bio lab we scooped krill into a jar.

We got a small fry pan, then melted butter and cooked up the krill.

Someone said, "Add garlic."

Somebody said, "How about pepper and salt?"

These were added. When the mixture looked ready, we ate it.

krill

"Tastes like butter," one person said.
"More like garlic," another said.
"Tastes like butter *and* garlic," Carl said.
"Krill don't have their own taste," I concluded.

December 21st
Palmer Station

A storm has raged for three days. A blast of wind smacked the main window with such force, we thought a bomb had gone off. The storm rose in intensity in minutes. Looking out the big window, we see a solid wall of sleet and blowing snow.

A friend and I checked the wind-speed monitor a few hours ago. It was clocking eighty knots. We decided to sneak outside and see what eighty-knot winds feel like. It's against the rules to leave the protection of the station in such high winds. Nobody saw us leave.

We were barely able to force the door open against the gale. Head down, face stung with driven sleet, I leaned with all my weight on the wind and did not fall over.

after the storm

Fearing I'd be blown away, I pressed my mittened hands on the side of the building.

We crawled on hands and knees, lashed by pellets of frozen rain. In five minutes we were back inside.

Thinking of the penguins and their chicks on Litchfield, I can't help wondering how many will die of exposure to the cold and wet.

Adélie chick

Midsummer Day, December 21st
Palmer Station

Dear T.,

Our cook is a young man with a great sense of humor. His socks, and all his clothes, don't match. He has earrings in his ears. He fixed a midsummer day feast of fried chicken, corn on the cob,

and watermelon. A tourist ship brought the fresh food in. Our meals are always good, but fresh food is rare.

The seasons are reversed in Antarctica. The astral spring and summer season begins in October, when the sun returns to the southern sky. At first it winks on for an hour or so. The days go by and its presence increases. By November it never sets.

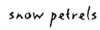

snow petrels

36

After midsummer day, the longest day of the year, the sun heads north and gradually vanishes for the winter season, beginning late March, or early April.

The play of light in Antarctica, all the colors I see, remind me of the desert at home. This desert is frozen, made of ice, fiercely cold instead of hot.

Off to bed with a full stomach and thoughts of home.
Love and XXXX,

Mom

The earth's axis is an imaginary line running from the North Pole to the South Pole. The earth rotates on its axis.

When it's winter in Antarctica, the South Pole is tilted away from the sun and Antarctica receives no light. When it's summer, the South Pole is tilted toward the sun and there is always light.

Earth's axis

sun's rays   Sun

winter in Antarctica

Sun   sun's rays

Earth's axis

summer in Antarctica

Christmas Eve
December 24th
Palmer Station

I t was three in the morning, bright outside, and I couldn't sleep. I crept downstairs, signed out, and took the flagged trail up the glacier.

Dressed in a watchman's cap, three layers under my parka, and Sorel boots, I climbed in a stillness broken only by the noise of snow crunching under my soles. Greenish-purple clouds covered the sky from edge to edge. The sea was the color of pewter.

Near the top I heard a cracking sound, a slap magnified a million times in my ear. Another followed, then another. Echoes of sound, aftershocks, sizzled in the air. The sky began to glow with an

front of glacier

eerie luminescence, as if someone in the heavens had switched on a neon light in place of the sun.

I felt myself dropping straight down. A crack had appeared under me, a crevasse in the glacier. Summer softening of the ice had thrown the pole settings off.

I'm alive because the crack was narrow. I fell to my shoulders, my boot soles too wide to fit through the bottom of the crack. I stared below into a blue-green hole cut with facets like a diamond.

After a few deep breaths, I began to scramble out. Terrified the crack would keep growing, I moved slowly. It was an hour before I was on firm ice.

The color of the sky
shifted to blue-gray
with streaks of
yellow along the western
horizon. To my horror, I saw a
pattern of cracks zig-zagging, like
fractured window glass, across the
glacier surface.

young tern

I checked my watch. I'd been gone three hours. I don't know why, but I didn't want anyone rescuing me. I decided to crawl down the glacier on hands and knees.

I felt my way inch by inch, rubbing the surface of the snow with my palms before making a move.

Back before the hour someone would have come looking for me, I told the station manager what happened. Trained in glaciology, he went up the glacier to reset the flags.

I have a new weariness tonight, born of having been

frightened out
of my wits while
watching one
of the most
beautiful skies
I'll ever see.

December 26th
Palmer Station

Dear S.,

gray gull chick

I read your Christmas letters over and over and pictured you opening the gifts I left behind. Our Christmas dinner was traditional, with turkey and trimmings. I helped decorate the dining room with crepe-paper streamers. People drew straws for giving gifts. I wrote poems to friends as presents. Without stores to shop in, people get inventive. One of the krill scientists, here with his wife who is also a scientist, wrote a sweet song for her.

On my way to bed Christmas night, I spotted a dish on the floor near the kitchen. It was filled with cat food. A small bowl of milk and a shoe box full of cat litter were next to it.

Adélie penguins

It was late, but the cook
was up. "Is that what I think it is?"
I asked, pointing to the cat dishes.
    "Yup."
    "Where's the cat?"
    "Out."
    "How did a cat get here?"
I asked.
    "She's my Christmas present from home."
    "I don't believe you," I said, eyeing him
suspiciously. "There can't be a cat here."

snow petrels

    "Okay, you're right, but don't tell. The scientists can be pretty
dull, thick-skulled you might say. My Christmas kitty is sure to
liven things up."
    I promised, word of honor, not to tell.
    Love, kisses, and Happy New Year,

Mom

January 6th
Palmer Station

Earlier today my friend Carl, the ocean scientist, came to my room and said, "Let's go see the green flash."

"The what?" I asked.

"Come on. You'll see. Hurry or we'll miss it."

We headed up the glacier, and at the top we sat facing west. The sun slipped slowly toward the horizon. As it fell, its orb glowed a deep orange. The shape of it was fat, like a

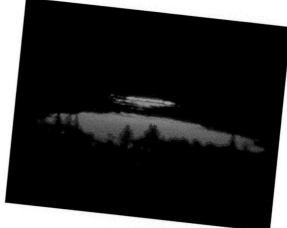

a green flash

squashed pumpkin. Near the end of the drop the light on top of the orb flashed green—the green flash.

"There it is," I said. "I saw it!"

The green flash is a rare, fleeting event in the earth's atmosphere. To catch it with the naked eye, there must be a clear horizon at sunset, as often seen over water. The green flash comes with certain conditions in the sky having to do with the way light bends. It lasts less than a twentieth of a second.

We started walking down the glacier, and Carl stopped me.

"Look," he said excitedly.

I stared and noticed that the surface of the sea near shore was a bright red-orange. The orange color was moving, as if someone had dropped a red sash into the water.

"A red tide," Carl said.

Hours later in the bio lab, Carl identified the organisms that caused the tide.

"Red tides are rare in these waters," he said. The organisms were one-celled animals, zooplankton, not toxic, which red tides often are. The tide lasted four days before currents carried it away.

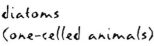

diatoms
(one-celled animals)

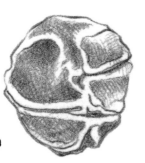

January 14th
A Ride on the Glacier

gray gull chick

New visitors arrive at Palmer—a New Zealander and a Britisher (nicknamed the Brit), geologists doing a survey of islands near the station. They offered me a ride in their snowmobile along the tops of the glaciers behind Palmer. I eagerly said yes.

We headed south, a mile above sea level, and could see mountains on the left, the glacier sweeping down to the Southern Ocean on the right.

We made a brief stop to check our bearings. For a moment bright sunlight broke through the overcast and streamed earthward. I looked toward the mountains and saw a mirage called the fata morgana, named after the fairy Morgana who built castles in the air.

snow petrels

fata morgana

Towers of ice hung suspended in the sky for ten or fifteen minutes, gleaming, shimmering turrets created by the angle of sunlight passing through ice crystals in the atmosphere.

The fata morgana is as mysterious as it is beautiful. No wonder it's named for the fairy Morgana.

Dear B.,

I took a walk south of Palmer, to a rocky ridge free of ice. It's a place I like to sit by myself and draw in fair weather. On the way I braved a skua "attack." Pairs of these birds defend territory by diving for your head. To present less of a threat, I crawl over their ground on hands and knees.

I found a perch overlooking a narrow bay. Sixty feet away, on the opposite shore, elephant seals basked, their ancient-looking, bleary-eyed faces prickly with whiskers.

I sketched with the sun streaming down, calm seawater reflecting light. After hours of this I felt sick to my stomach, feverish, so I headed back.

male southern elephant seal barking

southern elephant seals basking in the sun

Now I have the worst sunburn I've ever had. Blisters on my face are as big as fifty-cent pieces. My eyes are red, swollen, and runny. My head pounds.

There's no treatment but to stay indoors until I recover from being roasted like a marshmallow.

Much love, and wear a wide-brimmed hat when you're out in the sun!

Love,

Jenny

southern elephant seal

February 5th
Cormorant Island

Dear S.,

My favorite island, after Litchfield, is Cormorant, two and a half miles south of Palmer. The rocky shores and slopes are colonized by a species of cormorant called blue-eyed shags. They have blue eyelids and an orange salt-filtering gland on top of their bills.

The cormorants dive for fish in the sea. Their nests are made of seaweed and guano. Like penguins, pairs use the same nests every summer, so each year the nests grow larger, smoother, and, I imagine, cozier for the chicks.

Shag chicks are tall and slender, with thick down the color of burnished silver. I crawl close. They turn to stare, blinking blue-rimmed eyes. They are as much fun to draw as penguins. I love the lines of their graceful, long necks and pear-shaped bodies. My favorite birds after penguins!

Love,

Jenny

blue-eyed shag

blue-eyed shags

51

February 16th
On the Polar Duke

I am along on a trip on the *Polar Duke*, north of Palmer in Gerlache Strait. The crew and scientists trawl for krill using fine-mesh nets dropped off the stern.

Coming back we see icebergs drifting south out of the Weddell Sea. The bergs originate hundreds of miles away and ride ocean currents.

We sail close, but not too close, for beneath the waves is where the bulk of an iceberg is.

Seawater splashes up on iceberg shores shaped by years of wave action. Sunlight strikes gleaming ramparts that shine with rainbow colors. Erosion works at the ice, creating caves and hollows, coves and inlets.

Penguins and seals hitch rides on icebergs. Gulls and other seabirds rest on high points.

One iceberg collides in slow motion with another. The smaller one topples, rolls, and heaves like a dying rhinoceros, emerald seawater mixed with spray drenching its surfaces.

I yearn to ride an iceberg like a penguin or a gull, touching its frozen sides, drifting slowly on the waves. I draw them, but I can't capture their splendor.

February 23rd
Icebergs

Antarctic ice sheets are the largest in the world. Where the ice meets the sea, it forms a shelf over the water. Large pieces break away, making icebergs. This is called calving.

Icebergs are fresh water. When they calve, they move north, traveling on ocean currents.

Most Antarctic icebergs are tabular, flat on top. They may be sixty feet long, or two hundred. A giant bigger than the state of Delaware broke away in 1999. A tabular berg may rise eighty feet above the water, with five hundred feet hidden below.

Icebergs change shape as wave action erodes them and they slowly melt. The average iceberg drifts five to seven years before disappearing.

how glacier snow forms

snowflake   one week later   two weeks later   six weeks later

two years later   three years later   four years later   five years later

Ice just beginning to form is called frazil, made up of individual ice crystals called spicules. Frazil increases and becomes brash ice. Brash ice becomes grease ice. Greasy, soupy ice lumps join together into an elastic crust called nilas. Wind and water jostle the nilas, forcing the edges together into pancake ice. Pancake ice becomes pack ice twenty feet deep, solid through and through. Small pieces of ice are called frags, bergy bits, growlers, and floes.

"Galloping glacier" is one of my favorite ice terms. It means a fast-melting glacier that calves tabular bergs.

February 27th
Palmer Station

Dear T.,

Days for island hopping are dwindling. On Litchfield the penguin chicks pass through a brief, noisy adolescence. They are left alone when both parents go to sea to feed. There is safety in numbers from marauding skuas, so chicks huddle in groups called crèches.

Dependent on their parents for every morsel, they are hungry all the time. The adults return from the sea and are assaulted by famished babies, downy gray clumps screaming for a meal. Chicks chase any adult around the rookery, parent or not. They're big enough to knock the adults down. Adults sometimes turn in their tracks and race for the sea to escape being pummeled by a hunger-crazed chick.

Adélie rookery

a gentoo parent defends its chick from a skua gull

Now, with autumn coming, penguin chicks molt, or shed their down, and gather onshore before leaving the rookery to live on their own. The young are wary, nervous, forced by the shift of season to leap into the water.

An Adélie childhood lasts thirteen weeks.

Leaving the rookery for the first time is a rite of passage for the penguins. I wonder how many will end up in the jaws of the leopard seals I see patrolling the shores, anticipating the feast to come.

Much love,

Adélie chick

March 1st
Litchfield Island

My oceanographer friend, Carl, gets permission to visit Litchfield with me. On the island we see seals sunning on the beaches. Seals are hard to observe because they prefer swimming to basking.

Weddell seals

Seal babies, born on ice floes, are ready to be on their own after twelve or thirteen weeks of maternal care.

Tawny gray, equipped with teeth stout enough to chew breathing holes in the ice, Weddell seal babies soak up the sun's warmth before wiggling seaward to spend their first winter under pack ice.

*young
Weddell seal
sunning on
the beach*

Weddell seal under ice

On a gravel beach we approach a baby seal—not quite a baby since it weighs almost the same as an adult.

The young seal lifts its head and opens its mouth. I peer into the gape and retreat dizzily when the animal releases a cloud of smelly gas from its stomach.

It's a message to back off.

Watching the young seal, I try imagining what life is like under the ice in winter darkness. Weddells find their way and locate prey by whistling and clicking, making sounds that bounce off ice walls and echo back to sensitive receptors in their heads.

An old Weddell, with no teeth for chewing a breathing hole in the ice, is destined to die by drowning.

March 7th
Departure

shags on Cormorant Island

On my last day at Palmer, I went to Cormorant Island to see the shags. The sky was lemon-yellow with no clouds. The glaciers shone with soft, baby-blue lights. I drew for a while, then put my pencil down and wondered if I'd ever make it back.

I didn't want to leave. I hugged friends and cried.

The five-day trip across Drake Passage was stormy. The cook shut down the galley. Nothing stayed on the stove with the heaving and rolling of the ship. We ate cookies and fruit for three days, until the winds moderated.

SHAGS

Palmer Peninsula

It went completely dark the second night. I woke up
terrified, staring out the porthole in shock. It has been a
while since I've seen the darkness of night with stars
gleaming above.

March 12th
Winging Home

penguin egg

Before leaving, I collected (with permission) a sterile penguin egg that would never hatch. I made room for it in my suitcase by giving a lot of my clothes away.

The airline lost my bag in Miami. I told the airline people that I had to have it back, pleading, begging.

"It has a penguin egg in it," I said. They glanced at each other and eyed me funny.

Fortunately for me, and them, they found the bag.

The egg reminds me of my trip to the place where penguins raise downy chicks, krill swarm in numbers greater than stars in the sky, whales have rights, and icebergs drift in graceful arcs across Southern Ocean swells. At home, I'll look out at the desert landscape and remember the Antarctic desert, the last great wilderness on Earth.

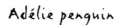

Adélie penguin

Bibliography

Bailey, Alfred M., and Sorenson, J. H. *Subantarctic Campbell Island.* Denver: Denver Museum of Natural History, 1962.

Barber, Noel. *The White Desert.* New York: Thomas Y. Crowell and Company, 1958.

Campbell, David G. *The Crystal Desert.* Houghton Mifflin Co., 1992.

Ceitelis, Jack (photographer), and Coloane, Francisco (text). *Antarctica.* Santiago, Chile: Ediciones Ceitelis-Rast, 1986.

Cherry-Gerrard, Apsley. *The Worst Journey in the World.* East Rutherford, N.J.: Penguin Travel Library, 1983.

Halle, Louis, J. *The Sea and the Ice.* Ithaca, N.Y.: Cornell University Press, 1987.

Harrison, Peter. *Seabirds: An Identification Guide.* Boston: Houghton Mifflin, 1983.

Hoyt, Erich. *The Whale Called Killer.* New York: E. P. Dutton, 1981.

Lofgren, Lars. *Ocean Birds.* New York: Crescent Books, 1987.

May, John. *The Greenpeace Book of Antarctica.* New York: Bantam Doubleday Dell, 1989.

Naveen, Ron. *Waiting to Fly.* New York: William Morrow & Company, Inc., 1999.

Naveen, Ron; Monteath, Colin; Roy, Tui De; Jones, Mark. *Wild Ice: Antarctic Journeys.* Washington, D.C.: Smithsonian Institution Press, 1990.

Neider, Charles, editor. *Antarctica, Accounts of the Journals of Admiral Richard E. Byrd, James Cook, Edmund Hillary, Ernest Shackleton, and Others.* New York: Dorset Press, 1972.

The Ocean Realm. Washington D.C.: The National Geographic Society, 1978.

Parfit, Michael. *South Light: A Journey to the Last Continent.* New York: Macmillan Publishing Company, 1985.

Pringle, Laurence. *Antarctica: The Last Unspoiled Continent.* Honesdale, Penn.: Boyds Mills Press, 1987.

Ray, Carleton, G., and McCormick-Ray, M. G. *Wildlife of the Polar Regions.* New York: Harry N. Abrams, 1981.

Sage, Bryan (text), and Hosking, Eric (photographs). *Antarctic Wildlife.* New York: Facts on File Inc., 1982.

Shackleton, Keith (paintings), and Stokes, Ted (text). *Birds of the Atlantic Ocean.* New York: Macmillan, 1968.

Spufford, Francis. *I May Be Some Time: Ice and the English Imagination.* New York: St. Martin's Press, 1997.

Watson, George, E. *Birds of the Antarctic and Sub-Antarctic.* Washington, D.C.: American Geophysical Union, 1975.

Wilson, Edward. *Diary of the Discovery Expedition to the Antarctic Regions, 1901–1904.* London: Blanford Press, 1975.

Wilson, Edward. *Diary of the Terra Nova Expedition to the Antarctic, 1910–1912.* London: Blanford Press, 1975.

Wilson, Edward (paintings and drawings), and Roberts, Brian (editor). *Birds of the Antarctic.* London: New Orchard Editions, 1967.